in Serving Jesus

*For Young Men:
Finding fulfillment in serving the Lord in adolescent and adulthood years.*

Vision Publishers
*PO Box 190
Harrisonburg, VA 22803*
www.vision-publishers.com
p. 877.488.0901 • f. 540.437.1969
email - cs@vision-publishers.com
We Welcome Your Response!

Joy

in Serving

Jesus

For Young Men:
Finding fulfillment in serving the Lord in
adolescent and adulthood years.

Samuel Beachy

Ridgeway Publishing
Medina, New York

JOY IN SERVING JESUS

Copyright © 2010 by Ridgeway Publishing

*To order additional
copies please visit your
local bookstore or contact:*

**Ridgeway Publishing
3129 Fruit Avenue
Medina, NY 14103
ph: 585.798.0050
fax: 585.798.9016**

ISBN# 978-098409854-5

Printed in the United States of America

Author's Note

The main character, Joseph Byler, and the struggles and temptations he faced in his youth are a combination of actual happenings to numerous individuals and situations. All names and certain details have been changed to protect privacy.

Table of Contents

Table of Contents..5
Introduction..7
1. Choosing to Follow God...11
2. Growing in the Lord..19
3. Maintaining Moral Purity..25
4. Prayer Life..33
5. Temperance...41
6. Used of the Lord...45
7. Accepting Advice...51
8. Being the Right Person...55
9. Being Open to God's Leading...59
10. The Danger of Fantasizing..63
11. Surrendering My Will to God's.....................................69
12. Persevering in Spite of Pain..73
13. Accepting Others...77
14. Finding Fulfillment in Serving God..............................81
15. Young Men, Be Faithful..87

Introduction

The heart cry of many Christian young men is to know God's will for their lives. But God doesn't reveal everything He has in store for us. Sometimes we might chafe under this uncertainty and try to push our way through life. But this only brings discouragement and defeat. God wants our complete trust and confidence, a complete sacrifice, a total giving up of our wants and wishes.

Those who choose to serve God by giving everything to him can truly experience *Joy in Serving Jesus*. Dear young man, if you do not have *Joy in Serving Jesus,* please give everything over to God. This is the only way you can experience true peace and joy. I hope this book can encourage you to do just that.

—Samuel Beachy

Chapter One

Choosing to Follow God

The bell rang and little Joseph Byler dashed for his desk. The rest of the children bustled about, trying to get to their seats before the bell rang the second time.

"Good morning, children!" called out the teacher in her cheery voice.

"Good morning!" they responded.

Soon joyful singing filled the classroom as songs rose from the children's lips.

All through school, the children were taught about the most Supreme Being: God. Year after year school went on. Many lives began to change as the pupils neared the end of their eight grades of education. They didn't know it then, but God was beginning to call them to leave their sinful lives and serve Him.

Often Joseph had heard "For all have sinned and come short of the glory of God."[1] He had also heard "Repent ye:

---
[1] Romans 3:23.

for the kingdom of heaven is at hand."² But as a child he did not understand these verses. The words "all have sinned" had gone through his young mind many times, but Joseph told himself, *I'm not really that bad...I mean, I've never done a whole lot of really bad things, anyway.* But even though he wanted to believe that he wasn't that bad, words like "sin" and "repent" gave him a funny feeling.

Joseph wasn't a carefree little boy anymore. The enemy had been busy over the years enticing Joseph and captivating his young mind. Now he was addicted to lustful thinking. But the Spirit of God had begun calling him. He had begun feeling guilty when he fed on lustful thoughts. He still enjoyed them, but the Holy Spirit was convicting him of his sin.

"Just a reminder: revival meetings are coming up next month," Brother James Mast, the bishop of Joseph's church, announced one Sunday. As a boy, Joseph had many times enjoyed watching people respond to the invitations at revival meetings, going forward and committing their lives to God.

Soon it was the first evening of the revival meetings. The Lord had been gently calling Joseph to come to Him. During the message, Joseph didn't feel convicted. But when the invitation was given, chills ran up and down his spine. *But I'm too young,* Joseph thought. *I'll wait till some other time.*

On Sunday evening, the last service of the revival

---
² Matthew 3: 2.

meetings, some of his classmates responded. Seeing people his own age respond threw his mind into wild action. The Savior was calling him, but the devil told him to just wait. *Don't worry, you still have plenty of time!* Joseph thought about the pleasure of his lustful imaginations. He knew that being a Christian would mean giving that up, so he chose to reject God's call and continue in sin.

Once the revival meetings were over, Joseph could enjoy life a little better—or so he thought. But a few days later his father, David, came to him and said, "Son, whenever you're ready to give your heart to God, please let us know and we'll pray with you." Joseph had an open invitation at home. His mother, Sarah, told him, "I'm praying for you, son." And the Spirit of God kept calling. But, oh, how he tried to avoid it!

Joseph still feasted regularly on impure thoughts, which led to fantasy and self-abuse. As Joseph kept on sinning, the enemy wrapped him tighter and tighter in his web. The more he fed on those thoughts, the more he wanted to think them. Joseph knew he should do what was right, but the devil continued to work, wrapping him up in the strands of his web. But the more Joseph tried to stop the wicked thoughts and lustful habit, the more entangled he got.

* * *

A year had passed, and again came revival meetings. Joseph was now under extreme conviction as Brother Dan

Lapp, the visiting minister, gave the invitation. It was a miserable week for him, and he couldn't enjoy anything. He could hardly wait for the meetings to end.

Joseph had been wrapped tighter and tighter in Satan's horrid web. Was there hope for him? Evening after evening, he remained bound. Joseph knew that he was lost and doomed for hell. But despite the leading of the Spirit of God, he hardened his heart even more. He still refused to surrender his will to God.

His parents were deeply saddened and disappointed every time he chose to reject God. Oh, how they prayed for him! Joseph's mother tenderly encouraged him to respond to God's call. Toward the end of the week, God used their love to begin to break his will.

Finally, the last evening of the revival meetings had come. Brother Dan preached the closing message and then gave an invitation. As the congregation sang the first verse of "Just As I Am," Joseph remained sitting.

His parents both watched him, knowing how he had resisted God's call before. David prayed, *God, please touch his heart. Please, Lord!* Sarah, too, pled with God. *Lord, help Joseph! Please bind the powers of darkness, and give him strength to respond to your call! I commit him to you, God. Please show him how sinful he is in your sight, Lord!*

The congregation started singing the second verse, and Joseph's parents prayed fervently for their son. Many others also prayed that the lost could find grace and strength to respond to God's call.

Joseph knew his time had come. He saw how filthy his sin was, and that it would bring destruction in the end. He could see that he was wretched and helpless, and that without God, he could never change, no matter how he tried. He slowly rose and walked up the aisle. Little did he know the great joy this brought to his parents and other believers in the church. His parents were overjoyed to see their son choose to follow God.

Brother Dan prayed with Joseph as he gave his heart to God. Joseph poured out his heart and prayed the sinner's prayer, "God be merciful to me, a sinner." Then Joseph prayed silently as he got up from prayer. *Oh, the peace and joy that flood my soul! Thank you, Father! Thank you God for saving a sinner like me! Such a priceless treasure!*

For a few weeks Joseph maintained a pure thought life. But Satan was enraged that Joseph had escaped his clutches. He tried with all his power to destroy Joseph's relationship with God. With time, Joseph fell back into the same lustful thoughts and habits that he had been delivered from. He lived in defeat, ensnared in the devil's trap once again.

I wonder if others struggle like I do? Joseph thought one day. *Maybe I should tell someone what is happening...No, they just couldn't understand. And then they'd know . . . I must be the only one that faces this type of thing anyways. And what would people think of me? I'd better not say anything.*

One Sunday, Brother James announced that the ministry would be open to starting a new instruction class.

His mother suggested that Joseph join. But he knew he had backslidden and needed to get right with God before joining instruction class; otherwise, he'd be a hypocrite. It took him a few weeks to decide what to do. Again, two roads lay ahead of him. He decided it was time to choose God. *God, I'm so sorry,* Joseph prayed. *You did everything for me, and look what I've done for you. I'm sorry, Lord.* Joseph got serious with God, seeking him daily in the Word and in prayer.

* * *

By the next spring, Joseph and three other applicants were ready to publicly acknowledge their commitment to God through baptism. Joy filled Joseph's heart on the morning of his baptism, but he also trembled as he thought of the great commitment he would be making that day. Could he be faithful?

"Young friends, the baptism you will receive today is an outward sign of an inward cleansing that God has already done in your hearts through your faith in the blood of Jesus. Now, you must press on and live out your faith in obedience to God. Fear God and keep His commandments," Brother James admonished. "Today is a special beginning, but we must all be faithful to the end. The prize is not at the beginning of the race or halfway, but at the end of our lives. You will be tempted by the devil many times, but be strong in the Lord; he can carry you through!

"If baptism is your desire, you may rise at this time,"

Brother James continued. "Joseph, are you truly sorry for your past sins? Are you willing to renounce Satan, the world, the works of darkness, and your own carnal will and sinful desires, and will you promise by the grace of God and the aid of the Holy Spirit to submit yourself to Christ and His Word and be faithful until death?" Brother James asked.

Joseph sensed a great burden of responsibility on his life. He had to renounce all sin. God must either be Lord of all or not Lord at all.

"I am," Joseph replied.

Yes, Lord, I am so sorry for my past sins. Lord, by your grace, I want to be faithful. Serving self does not satisfy. Lord, please help me to be faithful! I feel weak and helpless, Joseph thought.

"I baptize you in the name of the Father, the Son, and the Holy Ghost," Brother James continued, as water began to drip down over Joseph's head and onto the floor.

"God bless you, Joseph," Brother James said as he greeted him with the holy kiss. "I welcome you, and as long as you are faithful, you will be considered a brother in this church. The privilege of being a part of a church takes a life of faithfulness to God."

Joseph's fellow believers now called him a brother in the church, and he treasured the bond of kinship that he felt. It was a joyous day for his parents and the whole congregation. They were overjoyed to see Joseph choose to follow God. Later that day, Sarah penned the following

Joy in Serving Jesus

words in the back of his Bible: "I have no greater joy than to see that my children walk in truth."[3]

No, his battles were not over, but Joseph had laid a vital corner stone in his life.

Study Questions:

1. Why did young Joseph feel funny when he heard words like "sin" and "repent?"

2. What is one reason that Joseph found impure thinking so hard to give up?

3. What about baptism looked big to Joseph?

---
[3] 3 John 4.

Chapter Two

Growing in the Lord

Joseph found it such a blessing to be a part of the church. Before he was a Christian, he always tried to avoid personal questions. Now that Joseph was not living under the guilt of sin, it inspired and encouraged him when brothers asked about his life.

Jesus, through His death on the cross and His resurrection, had delivered Joseph from the grip of Satan. But the devil, furious with Joseph's choice to follow God, attacked him. Sometimes he failed, and sometimes he overcame. But he desired with all of his heart to grow in the Lord.

Joseph especially longed for growth in his speech. One day he read, "Let your speech be always with grace, seasoned with salt, that ye may know how ye ought to answer every man."[4] This verse really spoke to Joseph. He recalled how he used to often lash out at others with angry

---
[4] Colossians 4:6.

and hurtful words when things didn't go his way. Thankfully, though, it didn't happen nearly as often as it did before he was converted.

Joseph remembered one time in particular. He had gotten angry and talked harshly to his younger brother, Jason. Then he had realized that his mother was listening. Oh, how he had wished he could retrieve those words, but she had caught him in the act.

"Joseph, you know you shouldn't talk like that! I believe I need to wash your mouth out with soap," his mother exclaimed.

"Oh, no!" Joseph whined. But his whining was useless. He watched in horror as his mother diligently rubbed her fingers on a bar of soap.

"Son, open your mouth now," his mother commanded.

Those soapy fingers dug deep into his mouth, rubbing soap off as they went.

At last the awful process was finished and those uninvited fingers were out of his mouth. Joseph wanted to rush to the sink to wash out his mouth, but his mother didn't allow him to right away. After a little while, she permitted him to rinse out his mouth in the restroom. He washed out his mouth over and over, but the soapy taste was still there.

As a Christian, Joseph now saw what his mother had been trying to teach him. Back then it had seemed cruel to have his mouth washed out with soap. But now he realized she was trying to teach him a biblical principle. *Now I'm glad she did that,* Joseph thought. *If she hadn't, then I would probably struggle even more now.*

Joseph found that the Bible had even more to say about speech. "But I say unto you, that every idle word that men shall speak, they shall give account thereof in the day of judgment."[5] *Just what does it mean by an idle word?* Joseph wondered. He pulled out his dad's study guide and found the original Greek meaning for the word is "useless" and "barren." *So, this means I will need to give account for any useless or barren words I speak,* Joseph realized.

At first, Joseph thought he didn't use idle words. Then he thought about different times he had hurt himself. Those exclamations he had used were certainly idle words, and it had seemed so easy to speak them.

Joseph thought about how Jesus was mistreated at His trial before the crucifixion. But He didn't resist. He didn't even speak angry or vain words. Instead, He said, "Father, forgive them; for they know not what they do."[6]

Another time Joseph read, "The words of a talebearer are as wounds, and they go down into the innermost parts of the belly."[7] It reminded him of a hard lesson he had learned some years ago.

It had started so innocently. "Say, did you hear what the youth from Pine Springs did?" The word spread quickly. Joseph heard about it and passed it on to a couple of his friends. Then one day Joseph mentioned it to Brother

---

[5] Matthew 12:36.
[6] Luke 23:34.
[7] Proverbs 26:22.

Sam Bender, the deacon.

"Joseph, are you sure this actually happened?" Sam questioned.

"Well, Steve and Ben both told me about it, so I just assume that it's true."

Brother Sam had a special announcement that Sunday. "I called Jake Bontrager, the Bishop from Pine Springs about the news that has been going around about some of their youth. He said that they had checked into the situation and found out the whole thing was a rumor. Brothers and sisters, it's important that we only pass on what we know is true. If you have heard this story, please don't pass it on. If you have passed it on to someone already, please make the effort to clear it up."

As Joseph grew in the Lord, he found that words held great power for good, too. Once, Joseph's good friend Ivan Yoder, a poultry farmer, had faced a serious business loss. The heating system in the chicken house had malfunctioned when he was away from town for a long day, and by the time he came home he had lost thousands of birds. He was really facing discouragement, but God saw his disappointment and called on Joseph to be His message bearer. Joseph sent Ivan a card and wrote in it that he was praying for him. The encouragement was a real blessing to Ivan, and Joseph learned what a gift words can be.

* * *

A few months later, Joseph heard some shocking news.

His long-time friend and former school-mate Greg Sommers had turned away from God. He had left home and was living in Jonesville. How his parents and friends wished and prayed that he would repent and come back.

For years, Joseph and his friends kept praying for Greg. Would he ever come back? Joseph didn't know, but he hoped and prayed Greg would repent before he came to the judgment.

One day Joseph and some other boys got together to pray for Greg.

"Greg seems to think he doesn't even need God, like he's a good enough person without God or something." Joseph said.

"Yes," Kevin Helmuth agreed. "He's working off the foundation of 'the big I theory.' Satan was cast out of heaven because of his 'big I theory.' In Isaiah 14, Satan says, 'I will be like the most High.' Anyone with the 'big I theory' will end up in hell with Satan, don't you think?"

"Yes, that's right," the other boys answered. Joseph and his friends prayed hard for Greg, who had been raised in a Christian home but had chosen the wrong road.

Some weeks later, Joseph walked outside after dark and looked up into the night sky. Many stars were visible, and a thin crescent moon was setting in the west. As he continued gazing up at the clear night sky, he thought *Somewhere beyond the stars there is a God who cares about me. He sees me right now.* The presence of God felt so close.

It was almost as if he could hear the Lord reply, *Yes,*

child, I see you down there. I see you when you sin and when you are faithful. I notice when Satan throws his fiery darts at you. Remember, I will not allow the devil to tempt you more than you can bear. My child, even though life is hard sometimes, be faithful. You are only on earth for a short time. In light of eternity, life on earth is very short. So child, be faithful in this life, and I will give you the privilege of being with Me in heaven forever.

Study Questions:

1. How was getting his mouth washed out with soap a help to Joseph?

2. What are idle words, and what did Jesus say about them?

3. What lesson did Joseph learn about gossip?

Chapter Three

Maintaining Moral Purity

For years, maintaining moral purity had been a tremendous battle in Joseph's life, a battle in which he longed to gain total victory. Each defeat brought shame and discouragement. But he was sure other brothers didn't fail like he did, so he kept his failures to himself.

Then came youth Bible school. It was very encouraging for Joseph, especially the young men's purity class. He was especially inspired by singing "Purer in heart, O God, help me to be" with the other young men. Although he yearned for a pure heart, he knew it required a pure thought life.

"Young men, keep yourselves pure," Brother Ernest Graber admonished the young men sitting before him. "The Bible tells us that our bodies are temples that God dwells in. So, when we think impure thoughts, we defile the temple of God. And we have an enemy: the devil. Sometimes he walks about as a roaring lion, seeking to intimidate and then devour whomever he can. Now if we were out in the wild and heard a lion roar, it would make us afraid. It would be even worse if the lion stalked closer and closer to us, roaring louder and louder. But fear only makes us more susceptible to his aggressive attack.

"Sometimes we Christians experience severe bursts of temptation from the devil. It's as if Satan roars loudly as he attacks, hoping to intimidate and overwhelm us. The enemy throws a torrent of impure scenes before our eyes, and we struggle to maintain purity. But don't give up! Be faithful to the end of the battle, even when Satan comes on loud and strong. May God help us to sanctify our eyes and maintain a pure thought life."

Brother Ernest looked at his young fellow warriors, wondering if they were experiencing victory or defeat. He understood the battles that young men face and hoped that somehow he could help these young brothers.

"Young men," Ernest continued, "tonight we'll share our struggles and victories. We learn much when we open up and share together. We all struggle at times in the fight to maintain moral purity, so please feel free to share your struggles. We only grow when we're willing to acknowledge our weaknesses."

As the young men shared their hearts, Joseph discovered that others struggled in the very areas that he did. Like him, they struggled with controlling their eyes when they went to town, or with taking the second look.

Joseph was so thankful to know that he was not alone in the battle for moral purity. Sitting around him was a

Maintaining Moral Purity

group of young men who struggled with the same things he did. He now saw that the devil had lied to him, trying to make him think that he was the only one who struggled in this area.

He felt free as he confessed his faults to the other brothers. The battle was not over, but he seemed to have regained his footing. He knew there would be other battles ahead, but it was comforting to know that many other young men were in the same fight for the right.

"Young men, if we want victory, we need to confess our struggles to God and man," Ernest continued. "The devil wants each of you to think that you are the only one who struggles with impure thoughts. He wants you to think that you are different and strange. He wants you to feel useless and hopeless. These kinds of thoughts lead to discouragement and depression. When you share with others, you'll discover that you are not alone."

* * *

After Bible school, Joseph determined to regularly share with someone about his purity struggles. In spite of his best efforts, he was still not living in complete victory, and he knew that sharing with someone else would probably be a help. But he hated the thought of sharing those kinds of things with anyone else.

In time, the Spirit of God had his way and Joseph confided in Thomas Miller, a married brother that he really respected. Thomas then asked Joseph occasionally if he was maintaining moral purity. It was humiliating to confess his failures to another brother, but it helped him to stop and think the second time before indulging in impure thoughts. This accountability was a great help for Joseph.

Later, at another Bible school purity session, Joseph shared what a blessing it had been for him to share with another brother. After the meeting, the minister, Jacob Stoltzfus, explained to Joseph why being accountable to someone works well.

"It's not that the brother you share with has some special power of his own," he explained. "Sharing is a help because it helps us see who we are, and this draws our attention to God. Then, as we confess our sin to God, He forgives us and gives us strength to walk in victory."

As Joseph became more involved in the Lord's work, the devil tried furiously to destroy his relationship with God. Horribly impure thoughts kept tumbling through Joseph's mind, but he knew he had to remain faithful. He refused to let his mind dwell on those wicked thoughts. He knew the Lord had a work to accomplish through him.

Surely the intensity of this struggle is a reaping for indulging so deeply in impure thoughts in my early youth days, Joseph thought. *I now see that self is never satisfied. The more it gets, the more it wants.*

As he pondered the issue of impurity, Joseph remembered Brother James once preaching that impurity was like the dreaded disease leprosy. In Old Testament days, the Israelites forced lepers to stay away from the camp. Even their family and friends had to avoid them so that they wouldn't get leprosy themselves.

Leprosy may have started ever so small. But the infected area continued to grow until more and more flesh was consumed. The diseased person was stuck in a continuously downward spiral toward death.

"Evil thoughts, like leprosy, are also a downward spiral toward death," James had said. Evil thoughts lead to evil actions, and as with all sin, there is always a reaping. Joseph realized now that his years of indulging in impure thoughts and actions had given the devil a firm grip on his life. As a Christian, he longed for greater purity, but the things he had seen and done in the past still hindered his life.

Once Joseph came across this Bible verse: "Take us the foxes, the little foxes, that spoil the vines: for our vines have tender grapes."[8] As he read this verse, he knew that he had let the little foxes of impure thinking eat his tender grapes. This had brought devastation as more and more wicked, impure thoughts had defiled his young mind. As time went by and he continued to indulge in lustful thoughts, those foxes grew and multiplied. They became large hungry beasts, never satisfied, and always wanting Joseph to feed on more impure thoughts.

That is how it works—the more we give to Satan, the more he wants, Joseph thought.

* * *

---
[8] Song of Solomon 2:15.

Sometimes Satan came to Joseph in such a small, sly way. Other times, the enemy approached like a roaring lion as great torrents of evil thoughts poured into his mind. "Lord, help me to be strong!" Joseph prayed. "I need You so much in this temptation! I am weak and helpless!" He struggled to keep right thoughts, but he felt like Satan himself was pouncing on him. "Lord, somehow grant me release from Satan's grip!" Joseph pled.

The enemy continued to torment Joseph with ungodly thoughts. He knew that he must simply have faith that God would work.

You need to have faith in me, the Lord reminded Joseph.

Joseph was weary of Satan's continuing onslaught. "Yes, Lord, I trust you! Please help my unbelief!" Joseph cried out.

Then, in His mercy, God stilled the storm of thoughts. "Thank you, Lord!" replied Joseph, as rest and quiet returned.

Study Questions:

1. How was the group sharing time at Bible school so helpful to Joseph?

2. Why was it such a help for Joseph to have an accountability partner?

3. Why is it important to try to develop good thought habits when we are young?

JOY IN SERVING JESUS

CHAPTER FOUR

Prayer Life

Joseph found that in his struggle for moral purity, his prayer life was vital. When he was lax in praying, he struggled even more to maintain a pure thought life. Failing to read the Bible and pray daily seemed to weaken God's hedge of protection around him.

Joseph was inspired as he read about Enoch and Noah. The Bible said that both men walked with God and that Noah was a preacher of righteousness. *I wonder what their day-to-day walk with God was really like,* he thought. *How much time did they spend with God every day? How much time did they spend witnessing for God? How much time did they spend teaching their children about God?* Joseph figured that these men who walked with God must have spent a lot of time with Him in prayer.

Then Joseph wondered about his own life. *What kind of testimony am I for God? Do I really spend enough time with Him?* He wanted to do what was right, but it seemed that in his heart he knew he didn't reach out to God like he should. He purposed in his heart right then to sincerely reach out to God daily in prayer and in studying the Word.

As time passed, it seemed Joseph's prayers were more clearly and directly answered. *Why this change?* Joseph wondered. *You know what . . . it's been since I've been spending more time with God. I wasn't close enough to God before, so I couldn't hear when God spoke to me.*

Soon after that, Brother Sam explained in a message the importance of repentance in maintaining one's relationship with God. "A water pipe carries water from point A to point B," Sam began. "If the pipe starts to fill up with dirt, it restricts the flow. A partially blocked pipe usually doesn't unplug itself. Instead, it just catches more dirt until eventually the pipe becomes totally blocked. A blocked pipe means no water flow.

"Our prayer life is the same way," Sam continued, "The channel between God and us must stay open and free from sin. When this channel is clogged with sin, it brings chaos into our lives. We may think that we can sin just a little bit, like maybe a bad attitude or a proud spirit, and everything will still be okay. But every time we sin, we clog that channel between us and God.

"All Christians have different weaknesses. Some struggle most with their thought life, others with anger or dishonesty. Satan sees each Christian's weakest point, and he attacks right there, trying to get us to sin.

"We might think," Sam continued, "that just one more

look at some indecency, one small lie, or just one little act of disobedience is not too bad. But those who make excuses for so-called 'little' sins like this are on dangerous ground. These 'little' things destroy our relationship with God!

"We may run aground in our spiritual lives and wonder what has gone wrong," Sam explained. "We need to check our hearts. If we have carelessly indulged in what we tend to call 'little' sins, then sin has clogged our life and hindered our relationship with God. The water of God's Word can no longer flow through that channel and strengthen our lives.

"When this happens, is there hope to regain our relationship with God?" Sam questioned. "Yes, there is hope! We must come to God, confess our sins, and repent of our ways. 1 John 1:9 says, 'If we confess our sins, he is faithful and just to forgive us our sins, and to cleanse us from all unrighteousness.' Repentance is not just the way to become a Christian; it's also the way to stay a Christian! When we confess our sins and sincerely repent, the channel between God and us becomes unclogged. The water of God's Word can again flow freely."

Yes, it pays to keep our prayer channel clean, Joseph thought to himself. He knew that from experience, and he knew the devil was busy trying to clog the channel between him and God. *Dear God*, he prayed, *help me to never clog my prayer channel with sin. Please, Lord, help me to turn from sin and quickly repent when I fail.*

Joseph was always inspired when his prayers were

clearly answered. He recalled how recently he had looked and looked for his wallet but couldn't find it. Although he had felt sort of foolish to ask God to help him with such a small thing, he prayed anyway, trusting that God cared about even the small details of his life.

"Lord, you know where my wallet is," Joseph prayed. "Would you please help me find it? Please answer according to your will . . . in Jesus' name, Amen."

Once again Joseph started looking for his wallet, and right away he found it. "Lord, thank you for answering my prayer. Thanks for caring about my smallest needs, even though you are so great."

Thinking of the incident with the wallet reminded Joseph about the time their family van would not start. It was a cold winter morning, and the whole family was in the vehicle, ready to go to church. His dad turned the key, but all the starter would do was crank slowly. Things were looking bad. His dad paused a little and then tried again. Once again, the starter cranked slowly.

What are we going to do? Joseph thought to himself. *Do we need to take another vehicle? The car is too small to get us all to church.* Suddenly, for no mechanical reason at all, the starter cranked faster and the motor started.

Dad turned around as he was buckling up and asked, "Was someone praying that the van would start?"

"Yes," one of Joseph's sisters replied.

"I thought someone must have prayed!" Dad exclaimed. "The van wasn't cranking fast enough to start.

Something more than the battery made that starter turn the way it did."

* * *

The next year at Bible school, Joseph found out that the administrators had chosen to have a prayer and fasting session instead of lunch on Wednesday. Joseph thought this was strange. He saw no reason for it and hoped it would get canceled, especially since fasting usually gave him a headache.

But what seemed even stranger to him was that one of the brethren from the local church made a special effort to be there for the prayer and fasting service. He couldn't figure out why anyone would want to do that.

Joseph was not the only one who did not appreciate the fast day. Some of the other students made nasty remarks about having to skip a meal, and one rebellious student went out to his vehicle and ate some potato chips.

The Lord continued to work in Joseph's life and slowly but surely he began to appreciate fasting. One day he read how Ezra and the Israelites fasted and prayed.

Ezra and those with him wanted to travel from Babylon to Jerusalem, but to get there they needed to travel through hundreds of miles of unfriendly territory. The journey was long and dangerous, and many enemies might attack them along the way. They didn't know if they would even live to see Jerusalem. Ezra was ashamed to ask the King of Babylon for soldiers to protect them because he had already told the King that God would protect them.

There in Babylon, at the river of Ahava, they fasted, prayed, and asked God to help them. God did protect Ezra and the people, as Ezra said in Ezra 8:31b: "And the hand of our God was upon us, and he delivered us from the hand of the enemy, and of such as lay in wait by the way."

Joseph learned that God enjoys working in situations like Ezra's, when His children feel helpless in their own strength and turn to Him in humble prayer and fasting. He saw that God delights in taking impossibilities and making them possible.

It seemed to Joseph that when he fasted, the Lord worked mightily in his life. He came to see that fasting was much more than just abstaining from food. Fasting was something that made prayer very powerful.

Joseph sensed a need to spend much more time in prayer and fasting. The tasks and responsibilities ahead of him in life looked huge, and he knew that without God he was helpless. As time passed, things came up that seemed impossible at first. Yet as Joseph turned to God for help and strength, God enabled him to rise up and meet the tasks ahead.

The more he recognized his great need of God, the more God could work through him. Joseph indeed felt in great need of God's power. He thanked the Lord for His powerful work in his life, and prayed continually for the wisdom and direction he needed to continue in the Lord's work.

Study Questions:

1. What does sin do to one's prayer connection with God?

2. What is the value of fasting?

3. Is God most pleased to bless and help His children when they are weak, or when they are strong?

JOY IN SERVING JESUS

CHAPTER FIVE

Temperance

"Temperance affects every area of our lives," said Brother Stanley Coblentz during a Wednesday evening topic. "The Greek word rendered *temperance* here basically means self-control. We need temperance in every area of our lives. Working, playing, eating, and sleeping are necessary things. However, if we overindulge in any of these, we can lose control."

As Stanley continued speaking, Joseph realized that many times he put in longer work days than necessary, simply trying to make more money. He saw that he needed temperance in his work habits.

"We also need self-control in choosing our jobs," Stanley continued, "In considering a job opportunity, we need to spend time in prayer and seek counsel from others. Good pay doesn't necessarily mean a good job.

"We need to ask ourselves some honest questions. Will this job have a negative influence on my life? Will it hinder my relationship with God? Will I get so busy that I will not have time for God and my family? We need to use temperance in choosing our occupation."

From childhood, Joseph had really enjoyed fishing. Lately, it seemed he was dedicating more and more time to it. He didn't want to admit it, but he was becoming addicted to fishing.

As Joseph listened and thought about the time he put into working and fishing, he realized how easy it was to pursue those kinds of things and forget what he was here for. He thought to himself, *Why did God put me here on the earth? To be over-involved in my work and hobbies? No, God has me here to bring honor and glory to His name. In the light of eternity, only certain things will stand the test of time.*

* * *

One time during Bible study, Joseph read "For the drunkard and the glutton shall come to poverty: and drowsiness shall clothe a man with rags."[9] Joseph noticed that this verse listed gluttony and drunkenness in the same category. That meant that in God's eyes, drunkenness and gluttony were equally wrong!

In time, Joseph found that lack of temperance was nothing new. It had been a problem for thousands of years. In Numbers 11 he read how the children of Israel failed miserably in this area.

In the first part of the chapter, the Israelites complained

---
[9] Proverbs 23:21.

to Moses, asking him to give them meat to eat. Unthankfully, they had grown tired of manna and were longing for the fish, cucumbers, melons, leeks, onions, and garlic of Egypt. The Lord was greatly displeased with their complaining.

Later, the Lord sent a wind that brought quail. The quail fell in a three-foot-thick layer! The quail covered a vast circle a full day's journey around the camp in every direction. The Israelites spent all day, all night, and all the next day gathering quail.

The Bible says that he that gathered least gathered ten homers, or about seventy bushels. Then the children of Israel spread the quail out on the ground, probably as part of a drying method they had learned in Egypt.

God became very angry at the Israelites. He sent a plague among them and all those that had lusted after the meat died and were buried.

Joseph wondered how people could act as foolishly as the Israelites did. But as he honestly looked at his own life, he had to admit that he acted very foolishly at times, too.

Too many times I've overeaten, especially at the all-you-can-eat buffets. Sometimes it takes a few hours before I feel good again. It might be a good deal, but what do I really gain if I only feel bad afterwards and put it to my waist?

Lord, I'm sorry where I've failed in the area of gluttony, Joseph prayed. *Please help me be more faithful.*

Study Questions:

1. What are some areas in which Christians need more temperance?

2. Is a good wage the only thing to take into account when choosing a job?

3. To what other sin does the Bible compare gluttony (see Proverbs 23:21)?

CHAPTER SIX

Used of the Lord

As Joseph continued to grow in the Lord, God called him to encourage others by writing and by giving freely of his money and time. Joseph often sent cards of encouragement. God was faithful in showing him when others were in need.

A single young brother from Joseph's congregation, Mark Lehman, had done volunteer mission work in Honduras. The church had a sign-up sheet for the men to volunteer to write letters to Mark. One time Joseph was alarmed to see that no one had signed up for two weeks in a row. Joseph was surprised that there was so little interest in writing. Mark's family lived in another community, so he didn't find out news from his own church unless one of the brethren wrote to him. Joseph had just written Mark a month ago, so it really was not his turn to write. *Surely, with twenty-five brethren in our church,* Joseph thought, *I shouldn't have to write again so soon.*

But the Spirit of God won the battle in his heart. Joseph signed up to write that week, even though it may have been someone else's turn.

Time passed, and later Mark returned from the mission field. One day he told Joseph that over half of the letters he received from the congregation were from him. Joseph was shocked.

Joseph told Mark that he didn't fill up even half of the blanks on the signup sheet. Why didn't Mark receive more letters? It must have been that some of the brothers who signed up never took the time to write a letter.

One Sunday morning Joseph could tell that his good friend Amos Zook seemed discouraged. Joseph had a good idea why. Amos had been on the verge of buying his first farm when, for no apparent reason, the financing fell through. God prompted Joseph to write a card of encouragement to him. Right after church that Sunday evening, Joseph quickly made his way toward the back of the church and met Amos as he headed out the door for home.

"Here's something for you," Joseph said, handing him the card.

"Thanks," Amos replied, as he left the church. Later he looked at the card that Joseph gave him and thanked the Lord for His perfect timing in sending an encouraging message.

A few days later, he thanked Joseph for the card. "That card was a tremendous encouragement," Amos said. "It was really a gift from God. It blessed me so much that God cared enough about me to move someone to encourage me. Thank you for allowing God to use you, Joseph."

"Yes," Joseph said, "God just put it into my heart to give you a card. He's faithful, isn't he, Amos?"

"Yes, He is. Praise the Lord!" Amos replied.

* * *

Time had passed and Joseph was now of age. He had a job away from home that required him to purchase a vehicle. Once the vehicle was paid for, he started saving up money. It seemed that the Lord noticed his growing savings and wanted him to share it with others in need.

As Joseph continued to grow in the Lord, God showed him different people who needed financial aid. Joseph heard that Brother Jake Hoover's big family van had broken down. When he asked why it wasn't fixed yet, he found out Jake didn't have the money.

The Lord inspired Joseph to help Jake. He obeyed God's call and put a check for a few hundred dollars in Jake's mailbox. Later, Jake came to him with faltering voice and tears in his eyes, thanking Joseph for sharing.

Another time, Tim Hostetler was very sick and missed a month of work. Joseph knew that a month of missed wages would be a real financial problem for Tim, especially since he also had a doctor visit to pay for.

Joseph helped him out, and the Lord blessed him with peace for following His leading. A few weeks later he received a thank you card from Tim. Joseph was blessed as he saw how God moved one brother to meet another's need.

Joseph was fulfilling the scriptural principle of giving. Ezra 2:69 describes how the Israelites gave to the work of rebuilding the temple at Jerusalem. It says, "They gave after their ability unto the treasure of the work threescore and one thousand drams of gold, and five thousand pound of silver, and one hundred priests' garments."

The Israelites did not each give the same thing or the same amount of things. They gave according to their ability. The Hebrew word translated "gave" in the verse above can mean "restore." According to this, when we give to God's work we are only restoring that which is rightfully His. Everything we have is God's anyway. When we give as God directs, we are releasing back to God that which is rightfully His already.

One Sunday at church someone announced there would be a work bee the following Saturday. *Oh yes,* Joseph thought to himself, *I should definitely go and help.* Throughout the week, Joseph was busy with his duties. Then, on Friday, his friend Steve Keim asked him to go fishing with him on Saturday.

It would really be fun to go fishing again, Joseph thought to himself.

"I think it will suit me to go," Joseph said. "That would be great. Oh, no! Wait! I just remembered about the work bee scheduled for tomorrow."

Used of the Lord

"Ah, come on," Steve said, "don't worry about the work bee. There will be plenty of other people there anyway."

Joseph knew what he should do, but he also felt like fishing. He paused for a little bit and thought.

"Well," he finally said, "I already promised to go to the work bee. That's what I really ought to do."

The next day Joseph was glad he chose the work bee. *It sure is nice out here, working with the brethren,* Joseph thought to himself. *I would not have enjoyed my fishing trip anyway. Thank you, Lord, for giving me the courage to do what I knew was right.*

* * *

Once, when it was time for the yearly reorganization at church, Joseph entered the church house with an uneasy feeling. He was a little afraid he might be elected a Sunday school teacher for the coming term, and he didn't feel that he had time in his busy schedule to prepare to teach Sunday school every week.

"The intermediate Sunday school teacher will be Joseph Byler," announced the Sunday school superintendent, Joe Miller. As reality hit him, the task ahead looked great.

"Joseph," Joe said after the service, "may God bless you in the coming year as you teach your class. I know how it is to teach a term of Sunday school. It takes commitment to prepare for class each Sunday, but you'll find a great blessing in teaching as you put your heart into it."

The Lord continued to use Joseph for various responsibilities. The tasks weren't always easy, but when Joseph allowed himself to be used of the Lord, he was richly blessed.

Study Questions:

1. How is writing someone a card or a letter a way of giving?

2. Besides writing cards and letters, what other ways did Joseph find to give to others?

3. Joseph decided that if he had gone fishing instead of helping with the work bee, he wouldn't have enjoyed it. Why?

CHAPTER SEVEN

Accepting Advice

"What is the first thing that goes through your mind when you think of receiving advice?" Brother Sam asked. Joseph cringed inside at the thought of receiving advice, because to him it meant being told what to do. "Some hate to take advice because they are too proud to hear anyone else's ideas.

"Sometimes young people are that way toward their parents. Their parents' advice just doesn't seem to make sense. Maybe it even seems they are just plain dull and should listen to the young peoples' advice. But isn't it odd that such dull parents can have such bright young children?" Sam said, smiling. Others were smiling, too.

"When we go against good advice, we may well be putting ourselves in a dangerous position. And if things go wrong, what comfort and pity should we expect to receive? However, if we seriously seek God and take good advice, God will bless us with peace even if we face trials and difficulties. There is always a special joy in submission and obedience. Things may not go as we wish, but we can be at peace, knowing that God knows what is best."

Joseph could see himself in the minister's comments. For him, it was harder to take advice from some people than from others. It seemed easy to take advice from people he looked up to, but difficult to take advice from his parents and siblings. He liked to be the one who gave advice and told others how to live, but he cringed when others tried to give him advice. His tendency was to find fault with others when they would give him advice. Then he could feel justified in going his own way.

"What about before Communion services? When you express your peace with God and man, you say that you would welcome others to approach you about your life. But would you listen if they did?" Sam questioned. "Would you be willing to hear the person out—with an open heart?"

This really spoke to Joseph. Before each Communion service, Joseph, like the other church members, expressed his peace with God and man. He stated that he was open to the brethren to share with him if they saw something in his life that needed improvement. But as Sam spoke, he realized that in his heart he didn't really want to hear things about his life from anyone in the church. That meant that Joseph was lying about being open to advice! He confessed this to the Lord and asked Him to help him to humbly accept advice from others.

Accepting Advice

Later, Joseph decided to study the Bible to see what it had to say about accepting advice.

In Second Chronicles 10, the recently-crowned son of Solomon, Rehoboam, was seeking advice. The people of Israel had come to him and said that his father Solomon was too hard on them. They asked him to be kinder to them than Solomon had been, and promised that if he would, they would serve him.

First, Rehoboam sought advice from the old men. The old men advised Rehoboam that if he would be kind to the people, they would serve him faithfully. This was good advice.

Next Rehoboam asked the advice of the young men. They encouraged Rehoboam to tell the people that he would make life much harder for them than his father had.

When the people returned, he told them that instead of chastising the people with whips like his father had, he would chasten them with scorpions, or scourges. The message was clear: he would be a much harsher king than Solomon.

Rehoboam chose to reject the good advice of the older men and act upon the bad advice of the younger men. Because of this, the people rebelled against him. Rehoboam sent Hadoram, the revenue collector, to the Israelites who had rebelled, but they took vengeance and stoned him. Rehoboam, who had been in Shechem, fled for his life and went to Jerusalem. From that point on, God's people were divided. Israel and Judah became separate nations. There were bitter and long-lasting consequences for Rehoboam's rejection of sound advice.

Joseph saw from this Bible passage that being open to advice can prevent terrible problems later in life. "Lord, please help me to be humble and accept others' advice," Joseph prayed. "Please don't let me be proud and selfish like Rehoboam."

Study Questions:

1. Why do you think it was easier for Joseph to take advice from some people than from others?

2. In what way did Joseph find himself being dishonest?

3. What were the effects of Rehoboam's refusal to take good advice?

Chapter Eight

Being the Right Person

Joseph had been twenty-one years old for some time now. It felt good to pocket his paycheck, but now, he had to pay for some of the things that had always been furnished for him before.

He wondered what the Lord had in store for him. Would he grow to be an old bachelor, or would the Lord provide him with a marriage partner? Joseph didn't know where God would lead him.

"Be strong in the Lord, my dear young people," said Titus Beachy, the visiting minister. "You will never regret taking a stand for truth. When your friends want you do to something questionable, don't give in."

Throughout the youth message, Joseph listened intently as Titus expounded on God's Word. Titus looked out over his audience, wondering how many would remain faithful, and smiled encouragingly at the young people.

"Sometimes taking a stand and being faithful means little things. It's important to always be courteous and respectful toward others," he continued. "We should often use expressions such as 'please,' 'thank you,' 'you are welcome,' and 'I am sorry.'

"Youth are in a span of time between childhood and adulthood. Most of you do not want to be single the rest of your life. A normal young person will desire companionship. But many youth are too focused on finding the right partner.

"Finding the right person is not that important. You must focus on *being* the right person. God wants each of us to be the right person *for Him*. It is not so important to *find* the right person, but it is absolutely essential that we *are* the right person.

"Commit all your thoughts of courtship to God," Titus continued. "He can help you find the right person much better than you can. Just focus on serving the Lord and being the person He wants you to be. Leave your worries about companionship to God."

Later, as Joseph thought about the message, one thing kept going through his mind. *Finding the right person is not that important. I must focus on being the right person.* He had never thought about it that way before. He had been focusing too much on finding the right person. But now it was clear that he had been trying to get something to work out by his own efforts instead of waiting on God.

Joseph bowed his head and prayed, "Lord, I have

failed you once again. I'm sorry for seeking my own way instead of Your way for me. I'm sorry, Lord, that I haven't given my all towards being what You wanted me to be. Lord, I rededicate my life to You right now. Please forgive me and help me to be the right person. Help me, Lord, please, to be the person You want me to be."

God blessed Joseph as he strove to be the right person. Once, while busy with the duties of the day, he walked right around the corner of the barn and crashed into his younger brother Jacob. "Oops! Please stay out of the way, Jacob!" he said.

Soon after that, Joseph hustled into the kitchen to get a drink of water. His sister Mary was standing right in front of the cabinet where the glasses were. Without thinking, he tried to crowd her out of the way while reaching for a glass.

"Where are your manners, Joseph?" Mary asked. "You could have at least said 'Excuse me' and I would have gladly moved out of your way or even gotten you a glass."

Suddenly Joseph remembered what Brother Titus had spoken about in the youth message. He realized now that when he had collided with Jacob, he should have said, "Excuse me." And when he needed that glass, he could have told Mary, "Excuse me, I need to get a glass," and then waited for his sister to move.

Joseph saw that he needed much growth in this area. He wondered if he would ever grow up in the Lord as he had grown up physically!

But those who observed Joseph's life saw him growing in the Lord. They did not see a young man without struggles or who never made a blunder. But they did see a young man who was willing to say "I'm sorry," get up from his falls, and continue to serve the Lord.

Study Questions:

1. Which is more important for young singles: finding the right person or being the right person? Why?

2. Why did Joseph need to repent?

CHAPTER NINE

Being Open to God's Leading

Joseph pressed on in his Christian life, striving to be the person God wanted him to be. In time, he began to notice that some friends his age had begun courting. His heart yearned for a relationship as well, and soon he began to take steps in that direction.

One question haunted him: *Am I truly open to God's leading or am I following my own feelings?* Joseph knew deep down that he was taking steps towards courtship because of his own feelings. He simply did not want to be alone. He had started down the wrong path. He was not truly open to God's leading. He was following his own pursuits in life and running ahead of God.

Then one day Joseph read Psalm 37: 3-5. "Trust in the LORD, and do good; so shalt thou dwell in the land, and verily thou shalt be fed. Delight thyself also in the LORD; and he shall give thee the desires of thine heart. Commit thy way unto the LORD; trust also in him; and he shall bring it to pass."

Joseph could see that the psalmist was instructing the reader to give God his full trust and obedience.

He especially noticed the phrases "he shall give thee the desires of thine heart," and "he shall bring it to pass."

Joseph then wondered, *Is this verse telling us that when we commit our desires to God, He will bring them to pass?* As Joseph sought the Lord in prayer about the passage, he concluded that when you commit your way to God and accept God's way, then the Lord brings *His perfect way* to pass. It grieved Joseph to see that he had pushed ahead in his own way again. He poured out his heavy heart to God, "Lord God, I am so sorry…I have failed you again. I've been more concerned with my will than with yours. Please forgive me, Lord, and help me to seek Your will with all my heart. Help me not to run ahead of You ever again."

Then Joseph noticed that the first part of verse seven of Psalm 37 said "Rest in the LORD, and wait patiently for him." That reminded Joseph of the famous scripture in Isaiah 40:31 which says, "But they that wait upon the Lord shall renew their strength; they shall mount up with wings as eagles; they shall run, and not be weary; they shall walk, and not faint." In time, this well-known verse became precious to him as he learned to let go of his own will and wait on the Lord. He knew he was in God's will when he committed his future fully to God, and just rested in knowing that God was in control.

Joseph didn't know what his future held, and it wasn't

Being Open to God's Leading

easy to wait on God and see things continue to work out for his friends. But if God could best use him as a single person, he was committed to accept His will.

Study Questions:

1. Psalm 37:4 says "Delight thyself also in the LORD; and he shall give thee the desires of thine heart." Does this mean that if we love God we get what we want? If not, what does it mean?

2. What thing that is mentioned in Psalm 37:7 and Isaiah 40:31 is very important to staying in God's will?

JOY IN SERVING JESUS

Chapter Ten

The Danger of Fantasizing

"Fantasizing is sin!" stated Brother James bluntly. "We must discipline our minds. The mind left to itself will go into dreamland. Those who fantasize may think and dream about a certain individual for weeks on end. The more they feed their lustful imagination, the more it grows. Their mind is so full of imaginations that they are not open to God's will."

How true, remembered Joseph soberly. *The more I fantasized, the more control it had over me. Thank you, Lord, for what you taught me about the sin of fantasizing.*

It started by him imagining asking a certain girl for courtship. In his fantasy, the girl was overjoyed at his request and eagerly gave her answer. The fantasy continued, and they had their first date. They were both so happy, and things really clicked for them.

As they continued with courtship, things were going wonderfully. In Joseph's mind she became prettier all the time. They both looked forward to engagement and making wedding plans. Then came the big day when they were married. He fantasized about many happy details of courtship and marriage.

But there was also lust involved in his imaginings. He especially fantasized about the intimate things of life after marriage. He ignored the Holy Spirit's gentle calls and continued to feast on impure thoughts.

The more he fantasized, the more he wanted to. His carnal mind was never really satisfied, but always wanted more and more. Countless thoughts of married life with her raced through his mind.

Soon, he was almost constantly fantasizing. Joseph felt hooked and helpless. He knew he needed to stop these thoughts, but he had relished them so long he felt bound. Though deep down he knew he was sinning, he still enjoyed feeding on the fantasies. And the more he did it, the easier it became to ignore the Spirit's convicting voice.

A change began to take place in Joseph's life. His constant fantasizing began to drive him toward greater sin. He had a strong and growing desire to touch a girl. He knew that such contact belongs only in marriage, but the desire for touch began to drive him.

Joseph was devastated when another youth boy started dating the girl he had been fantasizing about. His secret hopes and dreams came to an awful halt. His mind spun, trying to understand this horrid reality. But even then, the fantasies he had indulged in for months wanted to

The Danger of Fantasizing

continue running through his mind.

Later, in turmoil, Joseph sought the Lord, asking why He had allowed something like this to happen to him. He could hardly believe that God would allow him to face such a depressing blow. Joseph was so hurt and disappointed that he could barely pray. "Lord, help me, please, somehow . . ." he groaned.

The Lord was about to show Joseph something that he did not want to hear.

My child, Jesus seemed to speak right to his heart, *this is your doing. You have brought this on yourself. You have sinned. Fantasizing is sin, just as much as any other kind of evil. You ignored the times that I tried to convict you that it was sin. I tried to show you, but you refused to listen. I knew where you were going, and, oh, how I wish you had chosen to follow My leading. If you would have, I could have kept you from all this.*

To follow me, you must be pure in thought. But you delighted in filthy thoughts and attached your heart to someone who was not yours.

My child, you must repent. You must see how sinful you have been and then come and confess before me. I know that this turmoil you have brought on yourself is painful, but you will find no rest until you repent. I will help you and give you strength and courage to continue, if you will come to Me.

Joseph buried his head in his hands and cried. He knew this rebuke was from the Lord, and he felt awful. His vain and foolish dreams were shattered, but most of all he had failed his Lord. He had sinned against God.

"Oh, God, I am sorry! I am sorry that I have so miserably failed you with this fantasizing. I know that I've turned my back on You and chosen sin. I see that this has cut me off from You, and I want to rededicate my life to You right now, Lord. Please forgive me! Help me, Lord, to be more like Christ. And, Lord, please give me strength to continue on."

Joseph found peace with God again as he prayed, but a bitter reaping followed. Over and over again, his mind sought to fantasize. Each time his mind tried to travel that direction, it would pierce his heart.

Joseph also saw that while he had been fantasizing, he had not been open to God's leading. His mind had been so consumed with evil thoughts that if the Lord had tried to lead him, he would have never seen it. God's leading would have never penetrated.

As the months passed, the reaping was no longer as severe. It had been a hard lesson for him, but now he clearly saw how sinful and devastating fantasizing was. He was determined to allow God to control his every thought and especially his pursuit of companionship.

Study Questions:

1. How did the problem of fantasizing begin for Joseph?

2. Towards what did Joseph's almost constant fantasizing begin to drive him?

3. Joseph was devastated when another boy began courting the girl he had been fantasizing about. Whose fault was his turmoil?

JOY IN SERVING JESUS

CHAPTER ELEVEN

Surrendering My Will to God's

Time went on, and Joseph felt the Lord had led him to notice a certain youth girl, Mabel Weaver. After fasting and praying about it for a time, he felt that his attraction to her was of God. He knew that it was time to ask advice from his parents. He knew he needed their full blessing before proceeding. He was thankful for the good relationship he had with his parents, and he hoped they might have some good pointers for him.

"What do you think, Mom and Dad," he asked, "is this something I should pursue? Would I have your blessing?"

David and Sarah were not sure what to think at first. "Well, Joseph," his dad said, "give us a little time to think and pray about it."

In a few days Joseph had his parents' blessing and so he went on to ask Mabel's parents for their approval. After a few weeks, he received a positive response from her parents, too.

Now comes the challenge! Joseph thought. He wondered what Mabel would think of his request for courtship. *Do I have a chance? Will she say no right away?* In the midst of such fears and questions, Joseph penned a short letter and sent it to her.

One week and then two weeks passed, and Joseph was kept in suspense. Different fears played back and forth within him. First, he feared her letter would not come at all, and then he feared it would come and dash his hopes.

"There is a letter for you inside your desk, Joseph," said his mom when he came home from work one day.

His heart skipped a beat and he hastened to his desk. The letter was from Mabel. Breathing a prayer of surrender to God, he gingerly opened the envelope and then unfolded the letter. The words "I do not feel led to start courtship with you," glared starkly at Joseph. He was stunned.

"Lord, you've led me to this point, and now the door is shut. Lord, was this a mistake? Did I misunderstand you? Or is there something wrong with me that she didn't accept my request? Am I not being faithful to you? What's wrong with me, God?" prayed Joseph with tears rolling down his cheeks.

In time, Joseph came to see that he had taken her answer too personally. He had been living a faithful Christian life, seeking God with an honest heart. As Joseph thought over the situation, he realized that he had his faults and imperfections like everyone else, but this was not why Mabel had refused him. As she had sought the Lord about it, she had just sensed that they were not compatible. He realized that some people, even though they are fine Christian youth, are simply not compatible with each other. But that doesn't mean that either of them is unfaithful to God.

Later, this same young woman started dating another youth boy. At first Joseph wondered why God let things work out for the other boy, but not for him. Years down the road, though, once he saw the choices the young woman made, he could look back and thank God for her refusal.

Joseph also noticed that some youth started courting and then quit. He came to realize courtship is a time of trial, a time for young people to become more familiar with each other. They need the chance to see if they are compatible enough to make that lifelong commitment of marriage. Some couples find they just aren't compatible.

We humans can't see the whole picture like God can. Sometimes we question how something can be God's divine will, but His way is always best for us. He simply wants us to place our full trust and confidence in Him.

Study Questions:

1. What was Joseph's mistake in relating to Mabel's refusal?

2. Is it a disgrace to stop courtship?

CHAPTER TWELVE

Persevering in Spite of Pain

Joseph woke up in the morning and everything seemed so bright and fresh. Peace and joy flooded his soul as he thought about God's goodness. Suddenly his joy faded and his whole world seemed to go dark and heavy. The phone call from the night before flashed through his mind.

"I just can't continue with our courtship," Sandra had said.

The last few months had been a joy for Joseph. After much prayer, fasting, and asking counsel and permission, Joseph had asked Sandra Gingerich for courtship, and she had said yes. Joseph had been nervous, excited, and happy all at the same time when he had first driven her home for Sunday dinner at her house. Their conversations had been a joy to Joseph. He had so looked forward to their ongoing visits and the time he would spend with her, and, just as he had expected, their relationship had been a blessing. He couldn't wait to learn to know her better.

But now, his recently begun courtship lay in ruins.

Joseph's desire to work vanished. Then, as he tried to cope with the sickening weight of it all, he suddenly remembered something.

Oh, no! Joseph thought. *I am supposed to have devotions at prayer meeting this evening! Why did the Lord allow the brother to select me to have devotions right in the middle of all this?*

Joseph shared his dilemma with another brother. The brother said, "God could have inspired the one in charge to get someone else. Maybe God wants to use you to show others how His strength can carry us, even during a hard time."

Thankfully, Joseph had already prepared notes for his devotions. As prayer meeting drew near, Joseph's mind began to clear. He spent extra time in prayer that afternoon, asking God to enable him to share His Word.

Later, Joseph sat in church as the congregation sang some opening hymns. In a few minutes, it would be time for him to have devotions. His grief was vanishing, and Joseph marveled to himself as he saw God take hold of his hurting life and use him to share His Word.

God demonstrated His power that night, blessing Joseph with calmness and peace. Joseph learned that the Lord does not want us to stay down from the knocks we receive in life. He learned to say no to self-pity and discouragement and just get up and continue serving God even when things didn't go his way.

Joseph thanked God many times for this experience. Each time, he was encouraged as he looked back and saw how God helped him. This showed Joseph so clearly that even when things seem to go wrong, God's power is always sufficient. This gave him courage to press on in following God.

Study Questions:

1. How did remembering Sandra's termination of their courtship affect Joseph?

2. How was the responsibility of sharing in Wednesday evening devotions a blessing in the midst of Joseph's sadness?

JOY IN SERVING JESUS

CHAPTER THIRTEEN

Accepting Others

Joseph had enjoyed going to youth activities for many years—until recently. It seemed to Joseph that a gray cloud had settled over the youth group, and he blamed it on the actions of an over-affectionate dating couple, John and Diana.

At youth functions, John and Diana seemed to be in their own little world, excluding others and barely taking a part in the activities. Because of his constant attention to Diana, John didn't take his responsibilities as youth leader very seriously. And, because of this neglect, youth group activities didn't seem to go as well anymore.

Joseph found the situation discouraging, and looked forward to the time when they would marry and leave the youth group. Finally, the wedding day came. John and Diana were married and moved on to another phase in life.

Joseph was much relieved once they no longer attended youth functions. *Good riddance! I am glad you are gone. Maybe now I can enjoy youth functions again,* thought Joseph.

In mercy the Lord spoke to Joseph about his attitude. *My child, you need to repent. You know in your heart that you have been unforgiving, hateful, and envious toward John and Diana, and you can never justify these sinful attitudes. You must be willing to forgive others, even if you don't like their actions. Although they shouldn't have acted the way they did, their behavior gave you no license to harbor such thoughts toward them. Your unforgiving and envious attitude is the real reason you have resented them so much and also why you could not enjoy youth gatherings anymore.*

Joseph was stung by Jesus' gentle rebuke. "Oh, Lord, please forgive me!" Joseph prayed. "I'm so sorry for harboring these awful thoughts. You are right, my own attitude is the real reason I've been so sour and discouraged. Please, God, help me to be more forgiving towards others."

Joseph realized that he had a bad attitude about the public affection of some dating and married couples. He wanted a special friendship as well, and he noticed when couples would touch one another in public. When he saw others indulging in their liberties, jealous resentment rose up in his heart.

How Joseph wished those couples knew how he felt when they touched one another in public, and that they would quit using their liberties like that. But he also saw that he must be very careful about his attitude. As wrong

Accepting Others

as excessive public affection was, his reaction to it had been just as bad. He had learned that other people's actions were no excuse for him to be resentful or unforgiving.

Study Questions:

1. What effect did John and Diana's excessive affection have on youth functions?

2. What effect did John and Diana's excessive affection have on Joseph? Why?

3. Was it right for John and Diana to act like they did? Did that justify Joseph's reaction to their behavior?

JOY IN SERVING JESUS

CHAPTER FOURTEEN

Finding Fulfillment in Serving God

"We can give everything to God but that one last thing," Brother James explained, "but if we cling to that one thing, then it will hinder our service to God. He wants absolutely all of our hopes, dreams, goals, everything. When we hold back, He does, too. But when we surrender everything, He blesses us to the fullest."

Over the years, Joseph had watched most of his friends get married. Some of his former youth group associates now had a number of children of their own. He continued to mingle with his married friends, but still attended youth functions even though he was quite a bit older than many of the other youth. He felt somewhat awkward at times, but a younger youth had encouraged him to keep coming to youth activities.

For many years and through many changes, Joseph thought that surely someday God would provide him with a life companion. As he grew older, the thought came to him that maybe God had chosen him to be single for life. At first, Joseph would hardly allow himself to think such a thing, but in time the thought came more often. When it came, he wanted to fight it. *No, surely God will send me a companion. He wouldn't ask me to be alone!* He didn't want to think of it as a possibility at all.

That meant Joseph had still had not given God his whole heart and life. He did not want to let go of his desire for a companion. As time went on, Joseph sensed he needed to surrender this issue, but it was a tremendous struggle.

What if I never have a wife? What if I spend all my days a bachelor? Joseph's flesh recoiled at the thought, but his refusal to surrender stole away his peace.

One time, the youth from Hillsburg came for the weekend. One of the chaperones that came along was Charles Hershberger, an older single brother. On Saturday the youth boys from both churches worked together to cut and split wood for Brother James. After the wood cutting, Charles rode with Joseph over to the church house for dinner.

After they had gotten to know each other some, Charles asked Joseph a tough question. "Joseph, are you at peace with the thought of being single all your life?"

"Well…it's actually a real struggle," Joseph said with a lump in his throat. "I just can't believe God would want me to stay single all my life."

"Joseph, I had a hard time with it, too, until I gave up,

just totally gave up. That's what you'll need to do to find peace, too."

Then Charles talked about how the Lord had greatly used the apostle Paul. "You know, Joseph, being unmarried provided Paul with freedom to travel and preach God's Word. I studied into this one time. Paul went on four different missionary journeys that each took a few years. He was away from home for a total of over ten years, plus the time he spent in prison! It wouldn't have been practical for Paul to leave a wife and children at home alone for months or years at a time while he went on his missionary journeys.

"He also experienced a lot of hardship and persecution in his travels. You've read about it, I'm sure. Four times Paul was beaten with many stripes, three times he was beaten with rods, and he was shipwrecked three times, too. He faced dangers on the seas and in heathen lands, by the Jews and by false brethren; he was at different times tired, in pain, hungry, and cold. His life wasn't an easy one, and if you think about everything he faced, it's clear that marriage wouldn't have been practical. If he had had a family, they wouldn't have been safe to travel with him.

"Another thing Joseph—while Paul was in prison, God inspired him to write many letters to the churches, and those letters speak to Christians still today. Paul was faithful in serving the Lord as He had called him. God used him in a mighty way as he surrendered himself to the Lord's working in his life. Joseph, you and I will probably never serve God the way that the apostle Paul did, but we each need to be fully surrendered to His will, whatever it may be."

Charles had given Joseph a lot to think about. Joseph saw how God used Paul, and understood that he must be resigned to singlehood if that was God's will for him. Holding stubbornly to the desire for a companion was robbing his peace and growth in the Lord. He needed to give Jesus his whole life. He had to surrender.

"Lord, I give up!" Joseph cried one night. "I commit my life and my future to you, God. Please take my life and use it to your honor and glory. I give you my desire for companionship. Do with it as you will, Lord. If you want to send me a companion, then so be it. And if you want me to remain single all my life, then . . . then, Lord, may your will be done. God, use me where and how you can use me best. I don't know what you have in store for me, but I give you my whole life. In Jesus' name, Amen."

This full commitment and surrender to God brought Joseph peace and joy like nothing else ever had. Although he had no clue where God would lead him, he was blessed with a deep and settled peace. He was thankful that he could experience joy in serving Jesus.

Study Questions:

1. According to Brother James' message, what is one thing that causes God to hold back blessings from us at times?

2. Whom did Charles use as an example of a single brother who mightily served the Lord?

3. How did Joseph finally find rest and peace?

CHAPTER FIFTEEN

Young Men, Be Faithful

Each of us must be faithful to God. Regardless of our situation, the Lord expects us to be fully surrendered and committed to Him. When we are, we will be happy and excited about life. Fulfillment comes by serving the Lord. Too many of us drag along, thinking that if we only had a certain thing, could do some special work, or were married, we would be happy. But true joy is a result of a vibrant relationship with God.

Singles have special opportunities, so they can experience many special blessings when they allow the Lord to use them. Since single men don't have the responsibility of being the head of a home, they are freer for service than married men. The responsibilities of marriage and family life take a lot of time. Singles have more time available and should use that time to work for God.

Young men who live at home do not have the expense

of buying or renting a place, and this enables them to give more of their finances to help others. They may be able to help young families that need some special assistance by sharing of their time and finances.

The Lord calls young men to do many things. Some help with work projects such as disaster cleanup and rebuilding, while others are schoolteachers at home or on the mission field. Others are faithfully serving the Lord while still living at home. Some serve the Lord by giving words of encouragement or a listening ear. Others are involved in writing poems, songs, articles, and books. Some focus on giving financial aid to the needy.

Since our talents and situations vary, so do our opportunities for serving God. But sometimes God calls us to do something that looks large. Our flesh cringes at the responsibility that lies ahead of us, even though we are sure that God is calling us to do it. If God asks you to do something, do it! God has power to make a donkey talk, and He also has power to help you work for Him. Even if we do not feel qualified, let's be obedient to God's call. We might be surprised how God works through us. Talent is not that important; God mainly wants our willingness to do His work. And a talent will do us no good if we are not willing to use it however God calls.

Sometimes single young men are too focused on future marriage plans and miss out on the blessings of serving God fully while single. And single men might have false ideas about marriage. They may think that when they find the right one and get married, the days of temptation will be over and life will always be just right. But they may be disappointed. If they have not learned to find joy in Jesus in their single years, it will not come automatically with marriage.

The devil will change his tactics after marriage. Before marriage, the enemy wanted the young man to touch the opposite gender. But after marriage he will try to come between husband and wife and destroy the relationship. The wife's faults will stand out and the husband will be tempted to not love her as a godly husband should. If that happens, Satan may in time try to entice the husband to take interest in another woman. So the battle continues after marriage, but the devil will attack in different ways.

Some youth struggle with loneliness and long for a special relationship with someone. Satan will often try to use that loneliness to cause them to sin. First, the devil may encourage impure thinking. Indulging in impure thoughts is sin, and if not stopped, it will in time bring spiritual bondage and destruction.

Second, Satan may encourage them to long to touch the opposite sex. The devil wants young men to think that intimate contact, even if it is outside of marriage, brings happiness. He tries to make them believe that they are missing something essential by not having a sexual relationship.

Those who give in to this thinking will go downhill spiritually and may eventually give in to sexual intimacy outside of marriage—a terrible sin against God and man. Then they will find that instead of happiness and fulfillment, sexual intimacy outside of marriage brings shame, guilt, and loss of relationship with God.

Young men, let's be faithful to God. Let us, by the grace of God, overcome Satan's temptations, because giving in to sin will bring us countless sorrows. God will bless us abundantly as we commit our lives to Him.

Faithful Christian youth are a tremendous asset and blessing in the church. They stabilize and encourage the entire congregation, young and old. Let's be faithful in serving God and allowing Him to lead us as we travel onward through life.

We older singles can be an inspiration to others if we are happy and fulfilled in serving the Lord. Others may know that it's probably our desire to be married, but they can be encouraged by our contentment in serving God however He has called us.

God wants each young man to experience *Joy in Serving Jesus*. May each one who has read this book find true joy in serving Jesus. True happiness and joy are a result of a fully surrendered and vibrant relationship with Jesus Christ. Let us faithfully follow God where He leads us.

Study Questions:

1. What are some unique service opportunities that single men have that most married men don't?

2. Does temptation end when marriage begins?

3. What are some common temptations faced by youth struggling with loneliness?